CLUE SEEKER

Clue Seeker

A Journey Back Through Time

to Search for an Identity

T. Owens Moore

Copyright © 2007 by T. Owens Moore.

ISBN: Hardcover   978-1-4257-8893-3
        Softcover   978-1-4257-8887-2

All rights reserved. No part of this book may be reproduced or transmitted
in any form or by any means, electronic or mechanical, including photocopying,
recording, or by any information storage and retrieval system,
without permission in writing from the copyright owner.

This book was printed in the United States of America.

To order additional copies of this book, contact:
Xlibris Corporation
1-888-795-4274
www.Xlibris.com
Orders@Xlibris.com
42186

Contents

Introduction 9

Chapter 1   The Adventure 11
Chapter 2   Great Expectations 13
Chapter 3   To Be or Not To Be African 15
Chapter 4   What is the Significance of Significance? 18
Chapter 5   From the Air to the Deep Blue Sea 21
Chapter 6   Land of the Lost 23
Chapter 7   Special Forces 28
Chapter 8   Ghost Man 36
Chapter 9   A Moorific Journey 39
Chapter 10   The Tour's Defeat 41
Chapter 11   The Anticipated Return Home 44
Chapter 12   Clue Seeker: The Transformation 46
Chapter 13   The New Beginning: Create Your Oasis 57

Epilogue 61

DEDICATION

To the beautiful butterflies
that exist in all of our lives

Introduction

Nostradamus predicted the doom of the world centuries ago, and subsequent catastrophic events have indicated the accuracy of his predictions. The Ancient Mayans predicted a change in the world by 2012. We are fast approaching this date, and the times in which we live are full of peril, evil, and deceit. The righteous are waiting for 2012 to usher in a new humanity. George Orwell wrote *1984* nearly fifty years ago, predicting the Bush administration's police state. Since the September 11, 2001 incident at the World Trade Center in New York City, life has become more oppressive for North American citizens. Orwell and other global thinkers foretold the Home Land Security documents and the Patriot Act. But who is paying attention? I became a clue seeker to try to understand my path. My experience can be a guide for any person seeking truth and their mission in life. No matter what gender, nationality, ethnic group, or culture, everyone is a clue seeker in his or her search for happiness.

It may be difficult for the metaphysical neophyte or less spiritually inclined to recognize past predictions. However, significant events that affect your perception of reality occur on a daily basis. *Clue Seeker* is not about predictions, but revelations. My experience will influence you to reflect on your own path and the signs and symbols in front of you.

In the decade leading up to the end of the Mayan Calendar 2012, two movies, *What the Bleep Do We Know* and *The Secret*, expose what *Clue Seeker* now attempts to reveal. The metaphysical world can affect our lives, and we need to tune into a cosmic consciousness to move forward. Unseen forces pervade the universe, and these forces can be harnessed to enhance our personal development. As you will see, everything is connected.

Clue Seeker is based on the true story of my travels across the globe. Names have been changed, but the story is a reflection of my life experience and it should guide others trying to understand life. When significant events occur, record them, and observe the signs and symbols that guide our lives. We are all searching for our purpose and reason for existence; identity is critically important.

Identity, therefore, is the theme of this novel; it affects every individual, every ethnic group, and every culture. In a globalized society, identity can be controlled and manipulated, making issues related to identity even more confusing. If you do not know who you are, then you do not know where you are going. As a clue seeker, I find more than I expect as the signs and symbols flash before me. We all have a mission, but we often fail to pay attention to the signs.

Clue Seeker will make you more aware of your mission in life as you pursue "happiness." Embark upon this journey with me and rediscover your true self. Life is a journey, and you have the power to define your own reality. Do not resist the signs and symbols that manifest in your personal life. Pay attention to the clues, follow your cosmic path, and watch how life's beauty can unfold.

Chapter 1

The Adventure

From 2000 to 2006, I had the opportunity to explore many regions of the globe—England, Spain, France, Portugal, Ghana, Brazil, Mexico, Jamaica, the Cayman Islands Virgin Islands, Puerto Rico, and the Dominican Republic. I thought it would be intriguing to document my travel to provide a look at my experience. My travels helped shape my view of multiculturalism and diversity.

The world is always changing, and it is important to keep up. As I began documenting my experience, I reflected on the European explorers who ventured to foreign lands. They were intrusive; many Europeans came to foreign lands believing in manifest destiny and desiring to control their environment and exterminate the natives. Many European settlers were xenophobic; they came in fear, while the natives welcomed the foreigners warmly.

As I traveled, I tried not to be the same as past invaders. My goal was to learn from new cultures and share my experiences. I hoped to have a fruitful experience. I met new friends and had unimaginable adventures. I walked the cities and countryside of Brazil, meeting people who knew friends of mine in the USA; I sat on a live crocodile in Africa, played in waterfalls deep in the heartland of the Caribbean, ate lunch in a cave in France, and jumped from twenty-foot cliffs in the Dominican Republic. I realized that others did not see me the way I viewed myself. I began to question who I was, and it has profoundly influenced how I see African people in the Diaspora. I had thought a collective African identity existed, but I discovered I was naïve. Miseducation and white supremacy have altered the consciousness of African people. No collective identity will exist as long as people neglect their roots. I spoke to numerous Africans born on the continent and was disturbed to find that I often knew more about African history than they did. They had authentic African culture to practice, a dialect to speak, and certain foods to eat, but they were ignorant of a pan-African view of history.

I will begin this adventure in 2004, with my trip to Africa, on a journey through time to search for an identity, for clues to guide my future. I trekked backward from freedom to the middle passage to enslavement on African soil to the mindset in Europe that created racism. Knowing your path frees your mind from oppression. We must learn to live and love life and to respect other cultures. The existence of humanity is dependent on new views, and this adventure will give insight on how conflict can be decreased as we focus on truth, justice, harmony, and balance.

Chapter 2

Great Expectations

The springing up of new housing complexes in the southern region of the United States gave me the inspiration to search for my roots. As the landscape is bulldozed, old trees are uprooted to clear space for cheaply made new homes. The image of a gigantic tree lying to rot is symbolic of the lost history of a people. Roots should provide strength and support for the trunk and branches. From the roots comes nourishment for the tree. Likewise, the roots or history of a people provides guidance and vision for the future. The uprooted tree is a reminder of the added "e" on my family name.

I was named "Moore," but I am conscious of the historical Moor who brought civilization to many parts of the world. I was never told about the Moors in school, so much of my history was neglected. I wanted to know if I could walk back through time and find remnants of the Moorish influence.

From reading history books in my adult years, I learned that the Moors influenced many parts of the world. The followers of Noble Drew Ali and the Moorish community carry on the tradition of the Moorish culture in North America. For example, we are told that George Washington chopped down a "cherry tree" with an ax. What is so profound about chopping down a cherry tree? In actuality, chopping down the cherry tree may be symbolic of removing the influence of the Moors from American history. The cherry-colored Fez and other symbols are examples of Moorish influence in American culture. Moorish influence can be observed in the Masonic world. I reflected on the treatment of Moorish history in many European-based colonial societies. Removing the black presence is necessary if people are to be socialized to believe that people of color are inherently inferior. "Uproot and remove" are systematic techniques to dismantle historical consciousness.

I wondered what I would uncover in Africa. The Moors had too great of an impact on world history for their history to be totally removed. It would be a costly journey, but restoring my uprooted history is priceless. I would search for a unified African consciousness. I would discover what I did not know about the world and myself. We should all desire to know our true selves in a world that destroys what it means to be human. I expect to find new perspectives. Take this ride with me as I embark upon a Moorific journey to find my personal connection to history.

Chapter 3

To Be or Not To Be African

From the beginning of this journey, I should state that I am Afrocentric in my consciousness. For me, to be or not to be African is the question. My ancestors were kidnapped from Africa centuries ago, and numerous social transformations have affected their descendants. The transformations extend from the various ethnic groups in Africa when brought to "the New World" to terms such as colored, Negro, black, mulatto, black American, Afro-American and African-American.

I will discuss being a free person in the New World on North American soil. I will travel back in time to experience the middle passage and return to where African people were captured. I then travel to Europe to see where the ideology of control and domination of people of color began. This trek backwards is a way to "Sankofa" our thinking into a new reality. If you do not understand where you come from and what your ancestral spirits have gone through, you will be lost in your search for self.

In my visits to other cultures, I have learned a lot about the world and myself. My story is written to guide anyone interested in truth and justice. This tale could have been a tragedy, but an evil spirit did not prevail. The ancient principle of "Maat," an African concept for truth, justice, righteousness, harmony, and balance, represented in Kemet (Egypt) in the form of a female god with wings was maintained.

On a metaphysical level, we are walking pieces of plasma. At the core of this plasma is the element that inspires right or wrong actions—Maat. As a clue seeker, I intend to restore a memory of Maat and to generate a new perspective on human relations. The experience can apply to anyone, any culture, and any ethnic group. To be or not to be who you are is a dilemma that all people experience. I have become awakened to new realities, and I would like my journey to be an inspiration for anyone searching for meaning in their life.

I have always been interested in how things worked. As a child, I used to dismantle radios and televisions. I liked to dissect insects and mix chemicals. When it came time to enter college, I was accepted into an aerospace engineering recruitment program. Engineering did not excite me, so I changed my focus and began to investigate the most elaborately constructed entity in the universe—the brain. As a professional psychologist, I am now in search of "the mind." This is my quest to connect to divine universal consciousness. It continually leads me to ask how things work, but it is futile to think I will ever have all of the answers. I will demonstrate how unseen forces, your ancestors, the God force, and the cosmic energy can guide you along a path towards personal freedom. When you fight the cosmic flow, you see resistance everywhere in your life. Learn to pay attention to your mind.

The human mind can create the universe and contemplate how the universe is structured. When we realize that everything in life is connected, it is simple to understand metaphysical experiences. As I tried to identify with a larger world, it became difficult to discern what was African, African-American, black, or Negro. Upon my return to the U.S.A., I observed tension in my home environment, debilitating the family spirit.

It took a major event to bring me to the reality that change was eminent. I was in a car accident on September 13, 2005, and this accident sent me through a "black hole" of cosmic experience. My life became transformed when I paid attention to the signs guiding me. I learned that our destinies are mapped and charted in the stars. For me, the number thirteen has provided guidance, but another sequence of numbers may be affecting you. The number thirteen convinced me that another reality guides our life, and when we fight the signs and the symbols, we go against the master plan. Life is about love and happiness and the imperfections of human behavior can interfere with the pursuit of happiness.

It is nearly impossible to achieve perfect happiness, but some have mastered the quest and obtained nirvana in silence and in darkness. In silence and darkness, you can meditate and channel your energy. Many people do not understand the harmonious nature of the cosmos, but my account should provide evidence that there is a connection to the cosmos.

On September 13, 2005, a driver hit me from behind while I was sitting in my car in a turn lane. The jolt sent me into another realm of consciousness. Try to visualize a concentric hole in the universe that can distort and/or merge your perception of past, present, and future, similar to a dream state. Our waking consciousness is an illusion. We are unaware of the metaphysical concepts that drive life. The black hole gave me a lesson in what it means to have a spiritual journey. The number thirteen symbolizes transformation. Follow me on this journey, which began in 2004.

Chapter 4

What is the Significance of Significance?

In the summer of 2004, the journey began on the fourteenth day of the month of my birth into the seen world. However, it is the unseen world, or the spirit world, that drives this journey. I awoke from a restful night with no worries about the day ahead. There was nothing unusual about the morning. The occupants of the house (wife, three children, and two visiting nephews) were preparing for the day, and I lay listening to the chitter-chatter of youthful voices.

I was preparing for my trek to Africa. My luggage was packed. The only thing missing was my family, for we could not afford for all of us to take such a trip. I was sad to leave them, but I knew they loved me, and the spirit that dwelled in our household comforted me.

On the day before my departure, the children were attending camp, and my second son Kali suffered a serious injury to the back of his head. He slipped in a puddle of water in the gym and slammed the back of his head on the tile. Normally, the children's mother Anika was available by cell phone, but for some reason, Kali's mother could not be located. Camp personnel fortunately reached me in the lab while I was training students how to conduct research while I was away. It was the busiest day of the summer. Why did the creator need me to attend Kali's emergency?

In reality, I should not have been available on my office phone that day; I was running late to go to my research lab at Clark Atlanta University (CAU), where I was scheduled to transport five research students to Georgia State University (GSU). The camp was at the Ousley Methodist Church in

Lithonia, GA. Serving as counselor was an ex-student, Tiffany Jay, who was in my college course during the spring semester.

Tiffany told Pastor Santos how to reach me on campus. They reached the dean of the School of Arts and Sciences, which generated a personal visit to my lab from the administrative assistant, E.J. Ryder, from the Department of Biological Sciences.

I reached the church in thirty minutes after I was contacted, and Pastor Santos recommended I take Kali to the emergency room. The back of his head was severely swollen. Upon my departure, I shared an audiotape containing two separate sermons I had delivered to two separate Methodist church congregations.

Pastor Santos had invited me to share knowledge with his Methodist congregation, and he was delighted to receive my audiotape. There was a surprising ten-year span between the two sermons (1994 and 2004) and the Book of Daniel was a common theme in both sermons. I had made the tape to give to someone else, but there must have been a reason for Pastor Santos to receive them. Perhaps I was led to the Methodist church that day by an unseen force.

Kali and I rushed off to attend to his injury. The doctor informed us that there was no concussion, and we were released from the hospital. I went home and fed Kali lunch, and went back to work with my son by my side. He had a chance to be with me in my travels to Georgia State University, Clark Atlanta University (CAU), Morehouse School of Medicine, and the Underground Atlanta Mall. He saw a hamster fight, a hamster surgery, and a science presentation from one of my students. He even received a necklace with an African pendant from a friendly proprietor in the Underground Mall. He met both new and old colleagues and forgot about his injury. The same day, I received a phone call from the CAU bookstore. They requested another copy of my book, *The Science of Melanin*, to place on their shelf for sale.

I had Kali carry the book and look inside to see to whom the book was dedicated. He did not remember that I had dedicated the book to him ten years before. What is the significance of this significance? My son, to whom the book is dedicated, carried the book to CAU's campus for sale.

On the following day, I was scheduled to depart for Africa. My spouse and I kept Kali home with us instead of sending him back to camp. It was difficult thinking about being away after Kali injured himself, but I knew he would be fine.

On July 15, before I departed, I stopped by a tennis court in southwest Atlanta. One tall, dark-skinned brother was sitting on the side waiting for four other players who were playing doubles. I asked if he wanted to challenge the winners. We warmed up together in the hot sun. When the four players finished their game, our potential opponents quit. The fellow and I played two sets of singles and chatted afterward.

His name was Ricardo Limon. I went to school with another Ricardo Limon at Lincoln University in Pennsylvania. The overlap in our lives was tremendous.

Ricardo had recently relocated to Atlanta from Philadelphia; I was born in Philadelphia. Ricardo was born in Brooklyn, New York, and my wife Anika was born in Brooklyn, New York. Ricardo graduated from Lincoln University in 1982. In 1982, I enrolled in Lincoln University, eventually graduating in 1986. A retired City of Philadelphia employee, Ricardo is enrolled in a graduate program at Clark Atlanta University for the upcoming semester. Ironically, I am employed by CAU, and I was born in Philadelphia. I am traveling to Africa for the first time, and Ricardo has visited five different countries in Africa. Rather than having Ricardo wait for his ride to pick him up, I drove my fellow alum home, and we had a stimulating intellectual discussion. What is the significance of this significance?

On my drive home, Lisa Clay, from the Department of Psychology at CAU just happened to be traveling beside me, going in the same direction. We began conversing through the open windows. We had not seen one another for several weeks, so it was catch-up time at 70 mph. We both got off at the same exit with ample time to talk at the stop light then went our separate ways. I went home to get dressed, see the family, and ride to the airport. I am in flight now, and I ask what the significance is of all that occurred on this fifteenth day of the month, in which I am about to travel for fifteen days in Ghana.

Chapter 5

From the Air to the Deep Blue Sea

Many modes of transportation can move us through the world. I mostly used airplanes. However, one trip on a cruise ship taken three weeks before my excursion to Africa reminded me of the horrors of the voyage across the Atlantic Ocean hundreds of years ago. I was in a cabin with five people. Travel was not always so comfortable. Now, of course, we were treated royally. We swam, danced, played paddle games, and ate whenever we wanted. We watched the sun rise and set and were mesmerized by the full moon glistening on the ocean. The ride was relatively smooth; you hardly knew you were moving. Many ethnic and cultural groups were represented on the ship, and people from all over the world mingled in a friendly manner, but all I could think about was how our ancestors were packed and stacked in the hull of the ship while the slave raiders rode in comfort. Periodically, the slave raiders allowed the Africans on the top deck for exercise and sun. I was taking the reverse of the middle passage. Our ancestors were brought over under horrendous conditions to a strange world, and I would be returning in luxury, cruising high over the earth in air-conditioned comfort.

Difficulty is guaranteed when embarking upon bold adventures, and the first leg of my trip to Africa was met with disappointment. I flew to Chicago to catch a connecting flight to London, which was to fly directly to Africa. In Chicago, however, the plane malfunctioned, we were delayed at the gate for four hours, and I missed my connecting flight to Africa. A brother named Emmanuel also missed his flight.

In the hours we spent waiting for an available flight, we became comrades in the struggle to free the minds of African people from the shackles of mental oppression. Emmanuel was actually a peacekeeper for the Ghana military. It was my pleasure to meet him, a warrior. He lived near where I was staying in Accra, Ghana, and he offered to transport me to my hotel when we arrived. The date was July 16, my mother's birthday. She birthed me in pain forty years ago, and I was having a difficult re-entry into Mother Africa. Is this significant? Do my trials remember and honor my mother and the Motherland?

Emmanuel and I found a flight on Ghana Airways; we were to depart later in the evening. There was no guarantee the plane would come, and no airline representative could confirm a departure time. We patiently waited and spent the time developing a friendship. The wait was reminiscent of the long wait for the slave ships to transport their human cargo, although our experience was more comfortable. When we finally boarded the airplane, we were packed in like sardines, just as our people were during the middle passage. The stench, the cramped seating, and the oppressive heat made me realize how mentally, physically, and spiritually debilitating a long ride could be.

My travel provided me a taste of the horrors of the middle passage and helped me find the significance in this part of my trip. My purpose was to first travel to Accra, Ghana, to participate in an educational tour of the experience of slavery with the Enyimnyam Project (E-Project), which was led by two prominent black psychologists, Drs. Naim Akbar and Wade Nobles. After my stay, I was scheduled to travel to Lisbon, Portugal to present biomedical research at the annual convention for the Society for Behavioral Neuroendocrinology.

Chapter 6

Land of the Lost

Most people know that I am a time conscious person. I am never without a watch. The circumstance that led to me losing my watch on day one of my visit to Africa was significant. My brothers from Ghana were entertaining me. We were sitting at a restaurant, eating, drinking, and being merry. When we departed the restaurant, one of the brothers asked, "Where is your watch?" My guide found it on the floor. A pin on my watchband was broken. I'd known it needed repair, but I had chosen not to fix it. Because I neglected to fix my watch, I spent the remainder of my time abroad without it.

The title of this chapter reflects the nine days of nonstop activity without much reflection on the day, hour, or minute. The schedule was exhilarating, and my mind was constantly stimulated, but I noticed a loss of mental consciousness in the minds of the native Africans I encountered. It is symptomatic of the troubles Africans are experiencing around the world.

In America, time seems to be a precious commodity. In Africa, currency is the most precious commodity, and it could be generated at any time of the day. Commerce happened around the clock, so time was irrelevant. What follows is a brief log of my nine days in Africa.

SATURDAY

I arrived at my room at 5:30 a.m., and I napped until 10:30 a.m. I awakened to videotape the city. I began taking pictures at the entrance of the hotel, which was near the main highway, and was astonished to hear someone call my name. Four men stopped behind me in a truck. I was shocked to see Emmanuel and his brothers. Emmanuel said, "Tim, get in,

I was just coming by to get you." We had not spoken that morning, and I just happened to be on the street. I had not eaten breakfast, and wasn't sure I had what I needed to be gone most of the day, but I jumped in the truck and was off to have my first adventure in Accra, Ghana.

They gave me a tour of the city and then we went to visit Emmanuel's family. It was pleasant to talk with the elders of his family. After visiting his family, we went to a restaurant, had a delightful meal at a community restaurant, and I broke my watch. After leaving the restaurant, we went to the beach.

Each stop we made, the "eat, drink, and be merry" philosophy of Imhotep was in the air. At the beach, we were provided with complimentary alcoholic drinks. By this time, it was about seven p.m., and it was decided to return me to my room and pick me up later to experience another section of the beach, where dancing and music was on the agenda. They came to pick me up, we stayed late, and my night was pleasant. I ate pizza and drank beer, and just as we were preparing to depart, I asked a couple of young ladies to dance. They both said no. I did not think much of it, but I was unable to reflect on the negative response until a few days later.

SUNDAY

Day 2 began with me being awakened by my roommate, T. Scott, from the E-Project, who arrived at 5:30 a.m. We were both battling time zone changes. He came in to rest, and I was on my way to tour the slave dungeons, but we took a moment to talk, brother to brother. I met Emmanuel's brother Thomas around nine a.m., and we caught a taxi to the bus depot. The experience was humbling. I felt like a sardine packed in a can, but I was a different kind of fish, and the others knew I did not belong. I did not know their real thoughts of me, but Thomas' presence helped comfort me.

We took the two and a half-hour journey to the Cape Coast. My guide was there, but he was unable to see the world through my eyes. The ride was rough, uncomfortable, and very unsafe. We arrived and took another taxi to the dungeons.

The dungeons were just as I expected. There is no way to describe the experience. All Africans should visit them, if only to ensure such horror never occurs again. We suffered a tremendous blow to our humanity, housed like animals for months. I also saw the pristine barracks that housed the white slave raiders. I wish I could have made the trip to the dungeons with my fellow E-Project members, but time was not on my side. I recorded video, took still photos, and etched in my memory what it was like in the dungeons of despair.

We left the dungeons at four p.m., but I was supposed to be back at the hotel by four p.m. for the E-Project reception. I missed the opening reception for the E-Project and did not arrive at my room until one a.m. the next day.

MONDAY

Day 3 was nonstop action. I had my first breakfast with the E-Project members. We were scheduled for a full day of activities. Our first task was to share in the Gifts of Splendor project. I visited a day care and helped beautiful African children, two to six years of age. After everyone completed his or her project, we went shopping in the city. We went to the W.E.B. Dubois Center to lay a wreath on the tomb of Dubois and then headed to Ebony Restaurant for dinner. The evening was spent at an African-American-owned jazz club. Coincidentally, the owner of the club had been employed at CAU before she moved to Africa. We did not return to the hotel until eleven p.m.

TUESDAY

Day 4 was the big journey north from Accra to Tamale. We picked up lunch in the city of Kumasi. We arrived at our destination ten hours after our departure, after visiting an African village and meeting with the village elders. Our elder, Nana Berko (Wade Nobles), explained the purpose of our mission, and they held a serious ceremony with libations, incantations, and two animal sacrifices. The experience was powerful for all who participated. We departed in good spirits, with blessings for a safe journey to Tamale.

WEDNESDAY

Day 5 saw another early start. We visited the Mud Cathedral in Navarongo. Beautiful children greeted our bus, and we went to the cathedral for a tour. We saw traditional African symbols, Islamic images, and the white Jesus representing Christianity. After leaving the Mud Cathedral, we visited the Nania slave camp and the "Rocks of Fear." This was an awesome scene because our travels shed light on the extent of our ancestors' exposure. They had no defense against the guns and fire used to capture them. This slave camp was deep in the heart of Ghana. If it took ten hours by bus to this region, how many days did it take to walk to the coast in shackles? We saw where the captives had to use carved holes in the rock as bowls. We saw the watering hole that served hundreds of captives. The expanse of land around the slave camp was overwhelming and reminded us of the freedom rudely snatched from our ancestors. We stayed long and poured libations on the newly renamed "Resistance" rock. It was actually called the Punishment Rock, but Nana Berko suggested it be renamed to honor those who resisted enslavement. Each of us left with a small rock in hand as a memento of the visit.

After departing the slave camp, we visited the Crocodile Pond at Paga. We took pictures of our mini safari and watched as crocodiles roamed where we walked. We took pictures sitting on a very large crocodile with extremely big teeth. Upon leaving the pond, we rode to the border of Ghana and neighboring Burkina Faso. We ate late and returned to our lodge for rest.

THURSDAY

Day 6 was the journey back to Kumasi, another long ride in our comfortable bus. I tried to avoid sitting in the same location every day. I wanted to know my comrades, so I made a special effort to converse with each E-Project ambassador in some capacity. Everyone was friendly to one another, and we all left with lasting friendships. We stopped to shop and to visit the Kintampo Waterfalls. We immersed ourselves in the water, which was spiritually rejuvenating. We relaxed from the whirlwind tour and returned to the bus. We arrived in Kumasi late that evening.

FRIDAY

Day7 began with a visit to Akwashio Kwahu, the traditional home of Nana Berko. We were warmly received at the village, where we were to establish a connection and provide educational assistance. Some members of the community believed money was misappropriated, and Nano Berko gave a speech to state otherwise. While we are subjected to exorbitant fees for private school and college in the U.S.A., our brothers and sisters in Africa only need $3 per year to send a child to school. With so small a donation making so great a difference, we all made an effort to contribute.

After leaving the village, we went shopping at the marketplaces. Everyone was tired, and we returned to our rooms late in the evening.

SATURDAY

On day 8, we visited Nana Bass and the Black and White Powers Shrine in Kumasi to meet with other African-American delegations to install a bronze bust of Dr. John Henrike Clark. This visit was significant. Our delegation, with Wade and Vera Nobles, Naim Akbar, and Marimba Ani, was powerful enough. Asa Hilliard[1], Leonard and Rosalind Jefferies, James Smalls, and Marcia Sutherland made an even greater impact. Nana Bass performed a traditional African ceremony, wished us a safe journey, and each delegation went its separate way.

We shopped and returned to the Gariba lodge at seven p.m. for a big celebration. It was my July 24, my fortieth birthday. I ask the question again, what is the significance of significance? Why was I in Africa for my fortieth birthday, in the Motherland with E-Project members? The festive evening ended with music and dancing.

SUNDAY

Day 9 was sad. I was scheduled to depart from the E-Project to attend a conference in Portugal; the other members were headed to the Cape Coast to visit the slave dungeons. It would be a spiritual and emotional experience, and I would not be there with my fellow E-Project members.

---

[1] Sadly, Asa Hilliard made his transition August 12, 2007 while attending a conference held by the Association for the Study of Classical African Civilizations in Egypt.

Chapter 7

Special Forces

There was no doubt in my mind before I left for Africa that we were in a war for the hearts, minds, and souls of African people. In a war, a foreign country is not where you want to be. Ironically, I exposed myself to a lonely escapade in the Land of the Lost. I was on a mission, and I took it seriously. What I should have feared is what I exposed myself to on the "dark" continent. I was an agent for the E-Project, involved in a secret mission.

Special Forces engage in covert actions; seldom is the mission revealed to other members of the battalion. My E-Project members did not know my early arrival and departure from the two-week E-Project mission was tactical. I was sent into Africa to covertly help rescue, reconstruct, and restore the minds of Africans in the Diaspora. The code name for the project was never revealed, not even to E-Project elders, but it was a 2004 version of the D.R.O.P. Squad [Deprogramming for the Restoration of Pride].

How did the U.S.A. and the C.I.A. kill Patrice Lumumba in the Congo, initiate a coup de tat on Kwame Nkrumah in Ghana, and spy on Malcolm X? Covertly, the government of the U.S.A. decentralized and destroyed any potential for a United States of Africa. In the same fashion, the Special Forces for the E-Project were challenged to fight in this war. Neither the elders nor the E-Project staff provided me with a gun, pistol, grenade, bow and arrow, rocket launcher, or even a stone. I was equipped with a weapon even more dangerous than the above—the mind of an educated black man.

I was thrown into the land of lost African minds. Fortunately, I was equipped with books and knowledge. When I arrived in Accra, Ghana, I felt like an alien in an environment where everyone looked like me. They did not see me as the same, so infiltration was difficult. The stage was set and the war was on. I could not reveal too much, but I had to give Emmanuel some information so he could help me revolutionize the lost African mind.

Then things got interesting: someone stole my identity. I knew Secret Service agents might accost me upon my return to the U.S.A., so I made a call to ensure I would not be hassled. I was surprised to hear the agent ask if I had been on a cruise a few weeks earlier. I confirmed that I had been, although I couldn't help but think, "They are watching me." I proved I was the legitimate traveler, so the agent called ahead and told the Customs officials not to detain me.

Unless tracked with a microchip received during my yellow fever inoculation, there was no way I could have been followed on my mission. I was in places few would dare to trek, I trusted my new colleagues, and I had confidence in sharing my mission with them. Emmanuel and his brothers became my first project, and it was a success, perhaps because Emmanuel was the spitting image of the late Dr. Khalid Abdul Muhammed. Khalid served as the minister for defense for the Nation of Islam and was the leader of the new Black Panther Party. I felt that the fighting spirit of our fallen ancestor was in the air; I just needed to work on his mind and soul.

He was in the military and completing a nine-month project in Texas, but there was much he did not know about our collective African experience. I expected Emmanuel to be conscious and prepared for the struggle. He was ready for a fight, but unclear, as so many of us are, on the issues. He knew who the enemy was, but did not know its full nature. After hours of lengthy discussions, I presented Emmanuel with a different view of the world. He was painfully limited in his understanding of pan-African history, but became fully engaged in my mission after the time we spent together.

When we arrived in Accra, Ghana, there was excitement in the air, and Emmanuel came to get me with his family and friends. He told his brother and two friends about the warrior/scholar he'd met, and insisted they be exposed to my African consciousness. Although they were all indigenous Africans, they respected my Afrocentric approach. We spent several hours engaging one another in conversation. Their minds were being opened and they wanted information. They wanted the weapons I had. I had their hearts, minds, and souls. The war was on, and it was going to be won.

The mission had tremendous success, and they escorted me to a world I never knew existed. I saw the hawkers (buy and sell addicts), the naked kids, the pot-holed, dirt streets, the outdoor toilets, the dilapidated schools, the plethora of shanty-town villages, and the lost souls and spirits of Africans relaxing and neglecting to worry about the rest of the world passing them by. It was evident that education was the key to turning around this social malaise, and that is what the E-Project elders have tried to do the last nine years.

As self-appointed commander of the Special Forces, I was in the trenches, like a European missionary peddling propaganda, to deprogram the malfunctioning minds of Africans trained to think like their British colonizers. These Africans knew virtually nothing about their history. On my mission, I went from project to project, single-handedly opening minds.

I survived day one and two of this secret mission. I was elated when the rest of the E-project troops arrived. I told them about the secret mission, but the E-Project elders had already provided them tasks. Together, we were ready to fight to liberate the minds of Africans from the shackles of mental oppression. For nine straight days, that is what we did. We successfully blazed from the bottom of Ghana to the top of the country.

On July 25, the time came for my departure from Kumasi. My E-Project comrades were scheduled to infiltrate the Cape Coast. I was to go to Lisbon, Portugal. Before leaving Africa, I engaged in a tactical mission to reach the coast from Kumasi without being detected, strategically positioned to reach a few souls before my flight out of the country.

On land, the E-Project crew traveled via the SunSeekers tour bus with Chief Kofi, who was in charge of the trip. They were leaving for the Cape Coast at nine a.m., and Chief Kofi arranged for a secret envoy to slip me out of town. It was so secretive that not even one hawker was outside the Royal Basin Resort when I departed. Chief Kofi's two corporals performed in excellent fashion to throw off any enemy combatants. They called at 6:30 a.m. and confirmed that they were prepared for the scheduled eleven a.m. pick-up. Surprisingly, not even Chief Kofi was aware of the covert activity, and his corporals swept me away at 9:48 a.m. No enemy would have been able to keep up with this final mission. I was alone, but I was not fearful.

The corporals drove me away, and I was alone in the heartland of Africa, where my existence could have been wiped out without a trace. If we crashed, got stuck, or were hijacked or ambushed by the enemy, no one would know, but there was a mission to conduct.

The head honcho, Corporal Braa Ofari, rode shotgun while corporal #2 drove. Inquiring minds began to percolate. Initially, the new soldiers were only inquiring about my travels. When it became apparent that they were not dealing with an ordinary black man, the discussion became more intense and the final phase of the mission commenced.

Time was short, so I threw out the bombs. Rather than a diatribe to stimulate their consciousness, I gave the head honcho two books to peruse in our short time together, the first of which was *The Moors in Spain*. He read in silence while I contemplated the potential fallout.

He knew nothing about black people who civilized Europe. "So how did they get to Spain from Africa?" It reminded me of what a white colleague asked me one day after an intense discussion, "So I wonder where white people came from." These were childish questions for adults to ask. It demonstrated the severity of miseducation that pervades North America and Africa.

Bomb #2 came in the form of *The Journal of African Civilization: The African Presence in Early Europe*. It blew Corporal Braa's mind. He thanked me for the experience. Once in Accra, he gave me a tour of the Kwame Nkrumah Center. I was grateful because Nkrumah was a fellow alum from Lincoln University in Pennsylvania. I wanted to pay my respect to the spirit of Nkrumah by visiting his tomb. My last Special Forces project on the continent of Africa was complete.

This last mission was a tremendous success. Brother Braa continued to ask questions and seek knowledge until my departure. In the ten hours we spent together, his consciousness was seared with the truth. I am convinced the war for the hearts, souls, and minds of African people will be won. Each E-Project ambassador is committed to create their own Special Forces and to get in the trenches where the lost souls dwell.

Pennsylvania, USA—Wissahickon High School track team photo (circa 1979) revealing the #13 on the jersey of T. Owens Moore. Moore is in the center position on the second row.

Ghana, Africa—T. Owens Moore standing above a live crocodile near a pond.

Ghana, Africa—T. Owens Moore and T. Scott standing in the midst of the Kwame Nkrumah Waterfalls in the heartland of Africa with Caprice Nassor in the background.

Lisbon, Portugal—The Moorish influence in Portugal can be seen in this photo of the famous bull ring called the Praca De Toiros.

Tours, France—The entrance to a cave in the mountainside of France where Moore and colleagues ate a meal. The cave has been constructed into a restaurant.

Sao Paulo, Brazil—T. Owens Moore meeting with economist, Ladislau Dowbor. Dowbor is the son-in-law of Paulo Friere, the famous Brazilian educator.

Salvador, Brazil—T. Owens Moore meeting with Tarry Cristina Santos, the educational coordinator at the Steve Biko Institute.

Chapter 8

Ghost Man

A black man's presence in a foreign land is interesting. In Africa, I felt like an ancient relic, like *Negrosaurus rex*. In Europe, I was a ghost. It was strange because many of my brothers and sisters in Africa had no joy in their faces when they stared at me. "Why are you here?" was the look I received, and I rarely went unnoticed. This is probably why no one danced with me when I attended a social gathering at the beach on my first day in Accra. After nine full days in Africa, I understand why I was ignored. My E-Project colleagues mentioned similar experiences.

In contrast, there was no issue in Europe. Black, white, yellow, red, and brown people all walked the streets, and no one had a problem with each other. I felt welcomed.

I came to Portugal to present my research at the annual conference for the Society for Behavioral Neuroendocrinology and got through customs without a problem. I tracked down a shuttle to take me to my hotel, and when I arrived, I was treated professionally. My conference reception was held that evening, and I found the affair to be typical. As in the past, I was the only black male participant from a black college or university. I should have stood out like a black bear in the Artic snow. At the reception, no one actually approached me, even though I recognized a few faces. I engaged in a few discussions and was received warmly. I even discussed Africa with an older white woman who had visited Southern Africa on a safari. She was not a neuroscientist, but attending with her husband. It was interesting that she was my first conversation at the reception.

The colleagues I knew did not recognize me during the reception. I was not hurt or disappointed because I understood the Eurocentric psyche.

From a Eurocentric axiological reference point, interpersonal contact is not an important goal. It was only strange because these individuals were researchers I have collaborated extensively with in Georgia. I spoke to them the following day, and one said he had not seen me, and the other made no special effort to greet me. Either way, had I been emotionally weak or had no cultural grounding, their responses would have bothered me. I simply went about my mission.

I was to spend five days in Portugal and only three were available for exploring the town. I had a presentation to give and attended other scientific presentations. Since I was a ghost, I knew no one would notice my absence; I was invisible. I slipped in and out and searched for the remnants of the African Moors who civilized this area of the world for nearly 700 years (711-1492 AD).

In the midst of my travels, the issue of identity kept surfacing. The words of Frantz Fanon echoed in my head: "Who am I? Am I really who I am? Am I all I ought to be?" I was clear whom I was and what my mission was, but I was in a foreign land.

As a human being, I identify with Africa. Although I speak of Africa and think of Africa, it is hard to be African in a world in which Africa is denied. Eye contact between similar people is common. On American soil, people do not hesitate to make eye contact and nod their heads to acknowledge the other person. In Africa, there was eye contact, but the energy was negative. In Portugal, there is no eye contact; people just keep walking.

On the issue of identity, it is apparent that who is to be and who is not to be an African is an issue. I can say African-American or "African living in America" when I am home. In Africa, I am an American or a black American. In Portugal, I am an American. In Portugal, I look like my African brothers and sisters, but they do not consider me a brother. Not a single African in Portugal engaged me in conversation. The ultimate barrier was the language. There was no hostility, but they had no interest in me. If I could speak fluent Portuguese, perhaps the reaction would have been different.

It was rewarding to see black Portuguese with black Portuguese, to suggest that there was a clear sense of identity. It was disconcerting that my identity was not strong enough to mix and mingle with my brothers and sisters in the African Diaspora. I felt with the African Portuguese much as I had with my white colleagues from Georgia, but although I considered them African, they were far removed from the African experience. What I observed in the bookstores helped to make sense of why I was nonexistent.

The Portuguese have systematically removed Africa from its roots. They convinced an entire nation that their greatness sprung from thin air. Think of how the Eurocentric version of history teaches that ancient Greece was the cradle of civilization. Even if one believes that, how could knowledge develop out of thin air? In both cases, the African roots have been deliberately removed.

I went to five different bookstores in Lisbon. I received the same reply each time. Since I did not speak fluent Portuguese, I would write down in Portuguese, asking about two topics: 1) slavery and human bondage, and 2) the Moors. I was greeted kindly and led to the history section. Three out of five stores had books on slavery, but none had any books on the Moors.

Miseducation is the key to manipulating the consciousness of a nation. I looked through many books, but I could not read the words. I purchased a large history book, *Os Primeiros Imperios* (*The First Empires*), one of sixteen volumes. I thought it would be a convincing example of how the Portuguese portray history. Although Egypt is in Africa, it was partitioned off on the map and the people in Africa were shown as white. This type of propaganda can have profound effects on the consciousness of the people.

This miseducation is similar to what I felt in Africa. The educated black man or woman living in America has access to the entire world. In our inheritance are the genes of the people who developed the first civilization. With our education, knowledge, wisdom, and experience, we are in a unique position to know how to win this war. Armed with knowledge and compassion, we can eliminate the ghost man phenomena and bring together Africans in the Diaspora.

Chapter 9

A Moorific Journey

The best way for me to begin this Moorific journey is to call on the words of Malcolm X from a 1963 speech to the grassroots, analyzing what he felt about the civil rights march on Washington DC. "When you have some coffee, and it is too black, what do you do? You integrate it with cream."

I find these words profound because this is what happened to the Moors in Western Europe. The Moors established the oldest city, called Alfama, in Lisboa. How could a people with such grand influence be written out of history? There was nothing on the Moors in any major book. I entered Portugal in search of ancestors, but the Moors were removed from the historical record. You might wonder, "Why is he so enthralled with the Moors?" Let me take you on a brief journey in history to help you understand.

Once upon a time, in the glorious age of African civilizations, black people ruled the world. This is no fantasy; proof of the African origins of civilization is overwhelming. The Shang dynasty in China, the Buddhist era in Asia, ancient Kemet, Mali, Songhay, and Timbuktu were civilizations influenced by Africans. The Indus Valley civilizations of Mohenjo Dara, Harrapa, Nubia, and Kush were all extensions of the black mind. During these eras, the recorded history of white people is virtually nonexistent. They were in the middle of the Dark Age.

The Moors were descendants of empire builders. They traveled to southern Europe during the early seven hundreds and left an indelible impression on the white European psyche. The Moors civilized Spain from 711 to 1492 A.D. They spread into Portugal and were close to conquering the southern region of France.

Dates, times, monuments, and artifacts don't lie. Untruths result when man interprets, falsifies, and alters the historical record. Do you wonder why people in southern Europe are darker than their northern counterparts? If dark-skinned black people continually mix with white people, the result is a brownish people with dark hair. Over 700 years of occupation, the African presence was stamped into southern Europe.

The expulsion of the Moors coincided with the white supremacist story of Christopher Columbus in 1492. Slavery and subjugation of dark-skinned Africans was the goal during this period in history. I was in Spain in 2001, and I visited Toledo, once the hub of the Moorish empire. I walked the streets of Lisbon and saw the bullring, which contains architecture influenced by the Moors. The King George Castle was supposedly where the Moors lost their last battle before retreating to Africa. Alfama is the oldest town containing Moorish architecture, but you would not know unless you studied your history.

I went searching for remnants of a people that awakened the consciousness of a nation. Portugal ruled the seas and eventually conquered Africa because of what they learned from their Moorish teachers.

Chapter 10

The Tour's Defeat

My African and Portugal trip ended in the summer of 2004. The day before my return was filled with excitement to see my family. I had never been away from my family for so long. Contact was minimal; we spoke twice by phone in the two-week period. It was a joyous return. I returned from my excursion filled with excitement.

In Madrid, Spain, I expected to see many ancient relics associated with the Moors. Toledo was supposed to be the educational hub of the Moorish empire. The Spain trip reinforced how history could be wiped out. From Madrid to Toledo, I saw little evidence of a black presence. I saw the carved head of a black Moor tucked away from sight in a cathedral, but these sightings would have to be pointed out by an experienced guide. The disappointment I experienced led to my search for an African consciousness in other cultures.

Two areas needed exploration to bring clarity to what I saw, so France (2005) and Brazil (2006) were next on the map. Europe presents a very different perspective on race relations compared to the USA. Many people of color are comfortable living in Europe. I was fortunate to present my research at the Collegium for African American Research in Tours, France.

For the conference, I titled my presentation "Moorific Journey" to discuss the horrors of the slave experience and my search for information on the Moors outside the confines of a book. What I found was startling. The Moors had a great affect on this area of the world, but the history books suggest that these were not people of African descent. In recent history, the identity of people of color has been defined by the minds of those who lack color. Around 1492, the course of history changed. I was curious to know how these people were expelled from Europe without a trace.

During my presentation, a white French woman gestured while I was presenting, and I couldn't tell if she was shaking her head in anger or agreeing with my content. At the conclusion of my presentation, a French speaking black man from Corsica expounded on the images I showed during my presentation. He explained that many of images of the Moors could be found on coins, flags, and carvings. Appreciation for African history and culture is difficult to comprehend in Europe. Many people of color feel comfortable there, but may not be fully accepted by the white population. In fact, in the classrooms, students in Tours hear about the role of Tours soldiers who defeated the Moors.

The woman in the audience making gestures during my presentation explained during the question and answer period that the grade schools in Tours teach the children to remember the Moorish expulsion. The people of Tours are very proud of their history as the people who repelled the Moors from Europe. I found this to be an interesting clue because this conference could have been held in any city in France, but it just happened to be in Tours, where I would uncover this information. My investigation was complete, but I wanted to know about the retreat and where the Moors went after leaving Europe.

My journey to Tours shed darkness on another reality that I never thought I would experience—cave life. Europe was tremendously different from Africa. I tried to imagine how black people could survive in so much colder an environment. I visited two castles and marched through the cold, dank stone creations. There were fireplaces, but it was difficult to see how they stayed warm and stayed clean without running water. The strangest experience I had was a visit to a wine cellar in a cave. I spent hours inside a cave, dining in a restaurant built into the mountain. There are no words to discuss about cave life until you actually spend time in one.

Initially, I thought of a cave as a carved opening in a mountain, in which people huddled together for warmth. What I saw in the European cave shocked me. The wine cellar was part of a gigantic cave system that had street names for the many corridors. It was so large that it was possible to be lost forever, especially without light. How ancient people survived under these conditions was amazing. I often feared I could get lost if I strayed from the tour group.

The black Moors surely did not spend much time in this region after they were defeated in Tours. European expansionism greatly affected their safety. They were forced to retreat from Europe to Africa and South America.

I had already been to Africa, so South America was my final search for the Moorish presence in world history.

In the next year, I was off to Brazil. The Portuguese colonized Brazil, so I thought it would be fascinating to learn what the African-Brazilians knew about their heritage. I returned to Georgia to prepare for the next exploration.

Chapter 11

The Anticipated Return Home

Many of the thoughts on my return from Europe and Africa were centered on how to convey my experience to friends, family, and the world. My family would love me as long as I remained true to myself. I did not plan to change, but my experience made me more understanding of race relations. Many of my thoughts were focused on how and when to make my experience public.

I had not found all of the answers. I did not know everything. I had to parlay my experience in a way that would not be intimidating. I had powerful videos and pictures, images that could help reconstruct, revitalize, and reaffirm an African consciousness.

I had seen the contrast between the Afrocentric and Eurocentric worldview. I experience an Afrocentric reality on a daily basis. Any contrasts are usually due to a head-on conflict with the Eurocentric experience. For example, while at the Society for Behavioral Neuroendocrinology conference, hugs and "soul brother" shakes were absent. When each speaker said good morning, there was no call and response. Most of the presentations were soporific and lacked the pedagogical instruction and oratory of black culture.

In the streets of Portugal, hawking or selling merchandise was performed in a secretive manner. In Ghana, aggressive hawkers bombarded consumers. Africa's hawkers, however, prepared me for a good deal in Portugal. The hawker dropped 300% off the original cost of an item, after I used the skills I learned from my brothers in Ghana.

Infrastructure, resources, and education are significant contrasting factors in the Afrocentric and the Eurocentric worldview. No one wants to discuss it, but the enslavement of African people (the MAAFA) is the sole reason for the disparity in the two worldviews. The MAAFA subjugated the

Afro-centric worldview and elevated the Eurocentric worldview. Africa is underdeveloped because of the diametric relationship between the oppressor and the oppressed.

On my return home, I thought of the millions of enslaved African people, the villages that were plundered, and the families that were destroyed. It is easy to imagine the chaos. I believe a sort of social amnesia, protecting us from contemplating our ancestors' suffering, contributes to our disconnect as a people. MAAFA is a term used by African-centered scholars to describe the experience. MAAFA has created the poor, dilapidated, undeveloped societies on the African continent. Conversely, Europe is developed because of the benefits reaped by enslaving Africans. Criminals created the "New World."

It is a crime to forget, and a crime for European perpetrators to not pay reparations. The international community should waive any debt that African countries owe the World Bank. Randall Robinson and others have written books about these issues, but the call has been ignored. Africa cannot grow and develop as long as the vampires suck its blood.

Why would supporters of a white supremacist ideology let Africa rise again? It would not be to their benefit. The solutions are internal. We need internal reparations before we can understand the destabilization of African countries. It may be wishful thinking, but African people in the Diaspora must create a collective identity. They are resilient, resourceful, creative, and intelligent. People of African descent set trends for the world, and changed and influenced numerous civilizations. With an accurate interpretation of history, people of African descent can begin to develop stable communities. Dr. Maulana Karenga (the creator of the African-American holiday Kwanzaa) said that the white man is guilty for who we are not, but we are responsible for what we ought to be. After my travels, I ask, who is the real enemy? On my return home, I see that the enemy is us.

I flew to Ghana and had a rap session with a brother. In Portugal, I had a rap session with a brother from Gabon. On my flight back to the U.S.A., I sat next to a sister from Senegal. The common theme in each discussion was that the media has helped form images of me that are inaccurate. I was trying to be African, and they were trying to be American. Many Africans I met identified with Americanism rather than focusing on their African heritage.

There is hope for people in the African Diaspora. It will take trust and commitment to change the world. I will continue to perform my Special Forces operations. Please join in the fight for the hearts, souls, and minds of the African people. I am aware that it is hard to trust one another. The enemy can sometimes sleep next to you. I became a Clue Seeker to put order to my house. Your personal house must be in order before you can rectify someone else's house.

Chapter 12

Clue Seeker: The Transformation

I returned from the Motherland with the feeling that something was not right at home. I did not know why my spouse showed no interest in the pictures or the video when I returned, or why there had been no interest in traveling with me on any of my trips abroad. There had been a lack of interest in my endeavors for the past few years.

Before September 2005, I had been unable to clearly put into perspective all the signs and symbols in my life. As a clue seeker, I was unaware of the meanings behind the synchronous events in my life. I am certain my car accident on September 13, 2005 was a sign from my ancestral spirits telling me to transform my life and show others what they can become. When you fight the cosmic flow, you see resistance everywhere.

September 13, 2005—Car Accident and Entrance into the Black Hole

Two days after the car accident, I was propelled onto a new road in life. The strings to my favorite tennis racket broke and my laptop computer crashed. I lost three years' worth of data and was scheduled to travel to Detroit, Michigan the following day. I needed the computer for my presentation. Needless to say, I had to make other arrangements. When I arrived to the airport, my Delta airlines flight was cancelled. I was assigned a new flight and seat number—seat number thirteen.

I arrived in Detroit for my conference and met a nice person who allowed me to use their laptop for my presentation. While sitting next to my new comrade, an Eric Roberson CD was ejected from the laptop. I saw this artist perform about five months prior. I sent forty books to the event, but sold exactly thirteen over the three-day period. On the Monday that I was to return home, my oldest son would be thirteen years old. Even more interesting, upon my return, Ticketmaster sent me an email to promote upcoming concerts. Eric Roberson was returning to Atlanta on October 13. A colleague brought to my attention that the area code for Detroit was (313). My birthday is 7/24 and 7+2+4=13. I was guided through the black hole with the keys to unlock a portal to the universe.

As I went through the journey, revelations kept coming. My marital disconnect escalated in the thirteenth year of marriage. I was interviewed on a local radio station, and when I was given the CD on which the interview was recorded, my voice came on in the thirteenth minute. I came out of class on October 13 and turned on the radio in the car. A spiritual advisor named Cheka Tuere was providing astrological readings for callers. I wanted more than a phone interview, so I called and made an appointment for the following day. The reading opened my consciousness. The number thirteen kept pushing me to change. Thirteen signifies change. My astrological reading ended at 10:13 a.m.

The experience in the black hole propelled me to seek a new journey. You may or may not believe what I experienced, but the evidence is documented. It does not matter, however, because you need to recognize your experience when you are connected to cosmic consciousness. When you resist the flow, you generate unnecessary mental, physical, and spiritual friction. Follow my flow, and I will show the cosmic force above and below.

Thirteen Signifies Change or Transformation

August 13, 2005—This date is retrospectively added to this journey because it signifies what I had been refusing to see for months. Despite my continued interest in my marriage, I received nothing but resistance from my mate and could not understand why. I legally filed for a divorce in the spring of 2005. My mate needed to explore what could make her happy, so I was willing to divorce as friends. She chose to be enemies. I was persuaded by friends to try to make it work. Marriage takes two people, and I needed to know why I was working alone. Believing my mate was sincere was the worst mistake I made. September 13 made me pay attention to the thirteenth year of my marriage.

In January 2006, I uncovered an article I had cut out of the Miami Herald on August 13, 2005, during the Association of Black Psychologists convention. I had received a call from my lawyer about a custody hearing date for the following week; my spouse had filed a counter claim to the divorce papers.

August 23, 2005 = 8/23/05 Add it together: 8+2+3=13. I went to sleep and dreamt that my wife was pregnant. It could not have been me. We had not been intimate in months.

Tuesday 9/13—The car accident. Neither my daughter nor I was hurt, but the accident slowed me down and put me through a black hole for a spiritual experience. I guess I did not pay attention on 8/13/05 or 8/23/05.

Thursday 9/15—The strings on my favorite racket break and my laptop computer crashes.

Friday 9/16—My flight to Detroit is cancelled. I get a new flight at the kiosk and the computer gives me row #13. The area code in Detroit is 313. In Detroit, I met a supportive soul (Marie). I see an Eric Roberson CD in her computer, which I borrowed to conduct my presentation. When I returned to Atlanta, Ticketmaster sent me an email about upcoming events, and Eric Roberson would be in town October 13. I sold exactly thirteen books in Detroit.

Monday 9/19—Javier, my oldest son turns thirteen. My 1992 Nissan Stanza is thirteen years old. My birth date (7/24) adds up to thirteen.

Sunday 9/25—On the CD provided for me from my radio interview, my voice came on in the thirteenth minute. Butterfly, a spiritual soul who crossed my path after the Melanin Conference in September, said she had been seeing butterflies and the number 313 was revealed to her in the shape of butterflies.

Wednesday 9/28—The new administrative assistant in the Department of Biological Sciences informs me that she contemplated whether to stay or go in her marriage of thirteen years.

Thursday 9/29—A graduate student from Louisiana called because my name was referenced in a book related to melanin. She tracked me down and left her home # and her brother's number. Both numbers had a sequence of 313.

Thursday 10/13—I left class and turned on 89.3 WRFG radio station. Cheka Tuere was giving spiritual readings on the radio. I set up an appointment to receive an astrological reading and it set me on a new path in life.

10/31 (13 backwards)—Lunch with astrologer Daniela at 1 PM (the 1300 hour). She recommended a website and I came across an article on planetary alignments. On Nov. 7, Mars would be in direct opposition to the sun. It would be bright at sunset and set the stage for the awakening for anyone paying attention.

Monday 11/7—This was the seventh week of a twelve-week marriage counseling program and the topic was "Forgiveness." On the seventh week of Radical Love counseling, my spouse revealed that she had had a lengthy affair. The counselor asked us to forgive and to work it out. Cosmically, the counselor's birthday is Nov. 13, and the zip code for where the counseling sessions were being held was 30013.

Sunday 11/13—I attended a meditation program at Tuere and Shayra's abode. I was the thirteenth and last person to arrive. I sat between Butterfly and

John (Daniela's friend). Pedro was there to lecture on the Mayan thirteen-moon calendar. I was reminded that the thirteenth letter in the alphabet is M. On the calendar, the thirteenth moon is called the cosmic moon and this is the month of my birthday according to the Mayan calendar. July 24, 2006 is the very last day of the cosmic moon month and 7+2+4=13. I felt compelled to leave a $13 donation.

Wednesday 11/23—Although I had a prepaid flight for Thanksgivings day, I decided not to travel. I ordered pizza and the bill was $10.13.

December 7, 2005—A spiritual advisor gave me a chakra cleaning. There was a massive revelation the following day. My ex-spouse's cell phone records were revealed to me, showing with whom my spouse had been having an affair. She had become emotionally, physically, and spiritually attached to another woman's husband. I watched the movie *Constantine* for the second time and there were more massive revelations: 1. My neighbor asked me to carry a gigantic floor mirror upstairs to her home; 2. A deleted scene showed that Constantine was questioned on 7/24/2003; and 3. Another scene showed the words "New Game" written on a bowling ball bowled down row thirteen for a strike. The significance of these three revelations is that a similar mirror was used to kill a demon in the beginning of the movie. My birthday is July 24, and the year 2003 was when my ex-spouse began her self-destructive journey. "New Game" and lane thirteen were subliminal reminders to move on with my life.

December 12, 2005—This date was the last class for the Radical Love Counseling Program. We were given an evaluation form several weeks prior to this last class. Question #13 on the evaluation form read as follows, "Rate your thoughts and feelings about marriage and your spouse, having just completed the course."

December 13, 2005 Is The First Day Of The Rest Of My Life.

January 4, 2006—Pre-scheduled physical with Dr. H. Powell. The receptionist and I begin a conversation and she tells me that her ex-husband's birthday was 7/24. While waiting in the lobby, I reading Chapter 13 from a book called *Fatal Flaws: Navigating Destructive Relationships with People with Disorders of Personality and Character*. During the visit, Dr. Powell and I discuss his similarly dysfunctional home environment.

January 13, 2006—Scheduled appointment to see a mental health counselor. The session was uneventful. After the session, I call a friend. It was a lengthy spiritual discussion and much advice about love, faith, and Jesus was shared. She had a different set of challenges in her marriage. She and her mate had not been intimate for thirteen years. On lucky Friday 13, I received my health report from Dr. Powell in the mail, and I am in excellent health.

January 16, 2006—My three children and I attended the annual visit to the Jackson family home for the King Holiday celebration. First revelation—I went to the room where the children were playing and played Lego blocks. While on the floor, I saw a book on the solar system in the thirteen-year-old child's room. I asked Khari to borrow his book to read while I was at the celebration. Second revelation—A brother from New York sat down next to me, introduced himself, and asked where I was from. I said Pennsylvania, and he actually guessed Penllyn. He began to talk about a fabulous woman he knew from Penllyn who died in 2001. It was my aunt, Dr. Cynthia Perry Ray. Third revelation—Upon departing the celebration, another beautiful spirit, Regina Sykes, blessed the kids and me with a hug and a prayerful thought before we departed. I told her about the universal connections because I had the solar system book in hand. She said the Sunday paper had an article about a new planet. I had bought the paper, but not read it yet. I went home, checked it out, and the name of the planet was:

2003 UB 313

January 18, 2006—The Brazilian consulate in Miami returned my passport with an approved VISA. The sender's zip code was 33130. My passport was returned to me with a stamped VISA to travel to Brazil in exactly thirteen days on January 31. The VISA was stamped January 13, 2006. I called two colleagues this morning, and while on the phone, Pedro from the WRFG radio station called me at 9:13 a.m.

January 24, 2006—I missed the Divorce 101 seminar; I rode around for an hour trying to find the location. I stopped to get gas at pump #13. Earlier in the day, I had looked into my files to recover my invoice for the purchase of my Toshiba laptop computer, which crashed before I went to Detroit in September 2005. Interestingly, I purchased the computer on June 13, 2002.

There was another retrospective revelation. I received national attention for my books on melanin when Tavis Smiley interviewed me. The tape was recorded November 13, 2002.

January 30, 2006—Read interesting "revelations" in Proverbs in the Bible. There are thirty-one chapters in Proverbs.

February 13, 2006—I had an enjoyable time at *Incognito* at the Roxy in Atlanta, GA. I saw a person I met two months earlier, at the Christian-based group counseling session. She served as a spiritual vessel to help my ex-spouse open up and deal with her lies. If it had not been for the counseling session, I would have never known her.

March 13, 2006—Venus was going retrograde. On this day, the Butterfly, Rainha T., and a thirteen-year younger soul (V is for . . .) opened my awareness to what beauty is and can be. This same month, *V is for Vendetta* hit the movie theaters.

April 4 to 9, 2006—(4+9 =13) I was in St. Thomas, Virgin Islands for a scholarly presentation with my thirteen and eleven-year-old sons. I left thirteen copies of *Dark Matters—Dark Secrets* with Will, who hosted my children and I for the visit.

April 13, 2006—I had a beautiful day. I realized I was doing everything to the best of my capabilities, and I had peace of mind. Unfortunately, I learned that my uncle/ father/ friend and tennis coach had an aggressive form of prostrate cancer.

Speaking of tennis, I made it to the playoffs for the Spring 2006 Kswiss Singles Tennis League. I was #21 out of 135 players. My plan is to win the championship. The numbers are in my favor. My record is 29 wins and 13 losses.

May 2006 is intense—I lost in the third round of Kswiss.

May 9—The ex-spouse no longer wants the house.

May 10—Settle out of court notification from my lawyer.

May 13—Computer battery dies on my Toshiba laptop computer.

May 14—Mother's Day and the thirteenth day of the Mayan calendar. Three mothers in the house for dinner, and the glass globe on the ceiling mysteriously shatters while we are eating dinner.

May 17: 5+1+7 = 13. My starter dies, the car stops, and my daughter and I are stranded ($700 repair) and $700 termite service. Parking space with rent-a-car at a restaurant was #17 on May 17.

May 18—I feel a new beginning. Noble Drew Ali (founder of the modern day Moorish Society died when he was 42). This book was completed when I was 42 years of age. Jokingly, I say Noble Drew Ali has reincarnated into Noble Tim Ali.

May 27—The ex-spouse tells the children about the divorce.

May 31—Birthday flowers are sent to "V is for . . ." for her friendship.

June 1, 2006—A comrade sadly revealed to me that his wife was having an extramarital affair. I did not believe him at first; I thought he was joking with me.

After reading the books my ex-spouse was reading in her leisure time, I realized why divorce had reached epidemic levels in the black community. You usually hear of men cheating, but there is a new wave of deception, and I am convinced that romance literature has helped ruin healthy male-female relationships. *The Woman of APF* is one book that says it all. A popular female writer called ZANE (she and her husband divorced in October 2005) wrote it. APF stands for "Alpha Phi Fuck'em." *The Woman of APF* is out of control, but it sells.

June 13, 2006—The ex-spouse finally moves out. The following day, the Butterfly informs me the lottery pick was 313. In the same month, my mother informs me that both my license plate and my phone number came out in the lottery. I did not play; therefore, I did not win.

July 9, 2006—I played in my first tennis tournament for 2006 and won first place.

July 13, 2006—The house is nearly remodeled to my satisfaction. This was the day before court mediation for my divorce. The solar seal from the Mayan calendar was the Yellow Warrior: ACTION-Question, POWER-Intelligence, ESSENCE-Fearlessness.

July 14, 2006—The mediation was a waste of time and money. She walked out of mediation instead of compromising. A lesson for life: never allow the clouded minds of others to determine your destiny. She is left behind in my mind; it is time to move forward. The solar seal from the Mayan calendar was my sign, Red Earth: ACTION—Evolve, POWER-Navigation, ESSENCE-Synchronicity.

July 16, 2006—Today is Queen Esther Moore's birthday—my mother. I made my journey to Mother Africa in 2004 around my mother's birthday and my trek to Mama Brazil around my mother's birthday.

July 17, 2006—I leave for Salvador, Brazil.

July 18, 2006—I meet two new African-American friends in Sao Paulo, Brazil. There was a change in my connecting flight, and I was lucky to have arrived early enough to find out. Some people were stuck in the airport in Sao Paulo for two days. There was only one flight per day going where I needed to go (Salvador). Even the flight I was supposed to catch was delayed. I met a retired brother from NYPD named Raymond and another brother named Ezeze who knows colleagues at Morehouse College. He has an apartment in the section of town in which I am staying. He even knows the Steve Biko Institute and people I know. These connections keep me in synchronicity with the cosmic force that is guiding me.

July 19, 2006—I meet a Clark Atlanta University student's father at the Steve Biko Institute in Brazil. His name is Dr. Paul Tiyambe Zeleza; his daughter Natasha was in two of my courses.

July 22, 2006—Today is Rainha T's fortieth birthday.

July 24, 2006—My birthday and the last day of the Mayan calendar for 2006.

Summer of Brazil Reflection

July 20, 2006, I go to the institute with an educator named Tarry. She is supposed to interview a visitor from the U.S.A. I saw new and old faces, and there was delight in the air. Only two people spoke English. One was Veronica, who was escorting the visitor. I introduced myself to the guest speaker. He is a professor at Penn State University. We exchange business cards and he tells me his daughter attends CAU in the psychology department. His daughter sat in front of two of my courses at CAU.

In October 2005, I met Tuere and Shayla, spiritual readers. Four months later in February 2006, I met Tarry and Sheila, two educators in Brazil. The names are spelled different, but they are similar, and Sheila and Shayla are pronounced the same.

While in Brazil, Varig Airlines collapsed. I was stranded. I was forced to find another flight two days later.

August 2006—The weekend prior to the final court date for my divorce, my two sons and I went camping in the North Georgia Mountains. We walked up Angel Falls and drank pure water from the mountain. After the court date, Tuere gave me a video to watch—*When Dreams Come True*. It was fascinating to see the parallels between this movie and my life and to see Angel Falls in it.

September 12, 2006—I took my two sons to the movies on September 12 to see *The Protector*; our movie just happened to be in theater 13.

On Wednesday, 9/13/06, the Butterfly was the first person to call me. It was a pleasant day. I chose to stay home and work. She needed a ride to the airport on 9/15/06, the same day I was traveling for the Sixth Annual Melanin Conference in Detroit. September 15, 2006

I returned to area code 313 for the melanin conference. The car accident had been exactly one year before, and I have seen a holographic representation of my life. I watched thoughts, ideas, and concepts merge into one. All I have asked for and consciously thought of has been created in my life. The presentation at the 2006 Melanin Conference would bestow information never before revealed to the world.

I settle into my room. I was supposed to have a room on the second floor. The receptionist changed it and put me into room 311. On the last day of the conference, there were thirteen scholars on the stage to receive questions from the audience. When I departed Detroit, I purchased gifts for my children. I gave the clerk a twenty-dollar bill and she gave me $13.03 in change.

I feel the power of the creator pervading my consciousness as I return to Atlanta. I give my colleague Bobby a ride home from the airport. On my way home, I get a call from the Butterfly for a ride from the airport the next day. Butterfly and I had not spoken since I left Atlanta. In Atlanta, I purchase a gift for my son for his birthday, and the gift is on sale for exactly $13.00. I purchase a cake for $13.25.

October 4, 2006

A high school friend who lived three houses away from my house where I grew up in Pennsylvania was killed in a car accident. He crashed on Route 13 in North Carolina. My nephew was killed in a motorcycle accident in North Carolina in the 1990s. In 2005, I was offered a faculty position at North Carolina A&T University. I did not accept the position. North Carolina has thirteen letters, and perhaps I was not led to this state to live.

The events that occurred near the end of 2006 continued to surprise me. I was to travel to Puerto Plata, Dominican Republic, October 5—8, to search for ancient slave sites scheduled to be preserved by the government. November 16—19, I was scheduled to present my research at a faculty research network conference in San Juan, Puerto Rico. I made my travel plans six months in advance for both trips, traveling during hurricane season. I did not encounter any bad weather and the people were lovely and beautiful in both places. Besides similar names, there were other interesting coincidences.

I made my plans six months ahead of time for both trips. During the U.S. Open Tennis Tournament in September, I called Jay Bernard, my college tennis buddy and mentioned that I was traveling to Puerto Plata, Dominican Republic, and he said he was going also. Even more of a coincidence, Jay stayed in the hotel adjacent to mine.

While I was in the Dominican Republic, I met a group of people from the U.S.A., and we went out dancing one evening. We danced and drank a little and watched the salsa and meringue experts step to the beat. While I stood to the side like a wallflower, I was swept onto the dance floor by a sexy lady in a red dress. My new acquaintances were amazed at the nice flow I demonstrated with her. It was an engaging dance, and I got a chance to show my skills while my friends looked on. The following day, a few in the crew went to the waterfalls and jumped from twenty-foot cliffs. It was an exciting exploration into a new land. I made it back to Georgia without problem. I even met a nice young lady on the plane. We had a delightful conversation. In our conversation, I found out that she lived in the housing subdivision next to mine. She kindly gave me a ride home from the airport. What is the significance of significance?

November 2006

The days leading up to my November trip to Puerto Rico were filled with other intriguing encounters. I bought flowers and a birthday card for the counselor born on November 13. This counselor assisted my ex-spouse with her secret life. The day I delivered the flowers and card, I called Ezeze just to say hello, and he told me that his birthday was November 13. What is the significance of significance?

On November 15, the day before I was to leave for Puerto Rico my oldest son needed to go the emergency room for a potential broken toe. Two years prior, I was in the hospital emergency room with my second son for a head injury. Both events were completely separate in space and time. Everything began to come in twos. Lisa Clay from the Department of Psychology and I do not cross paths often, but I happened to see her the day before I left for Africa in July 2004. She called me this day before I was to depart the country. Lisa was no longer employed by CAU, and we had not talked in months. In addition, I was contacted by two very important souls in my life who had helped to redefine my view of positive male/female relationships. I received a call from Rainha T in the morning and I saw the Butterfly on the evening of November 15. What is the significance of significance?

For the trip to Puerto Rico on November 16, I was in seat 13G and was shocked to see a colleague from CAU arrive. I did not realize Constance Chapman was scheduled to present at the Faculty Resource Network and was amazed that we had seats next to one another on the airplane. Two additional colleagues, Janice Liddell and Vicki Mack, were also attending the conference.

There were over 250 participants in this conference. At the reception at Sacred Heart University, a young group of entertainers entertained us. I was swept onto the floor by one of the dancers. My colleagues were amazed at my salsa and meringue moves. Later in the evening, there was a dance contest. I won the vote for the best male dancer. One month earlier, I had been doing Latin-style dances in the Dominican Republic.

When I returned from Puerto Rico, the car I had been driving all through my marriage would no longer go in reverse. It was a vivid reminder to always move forward in life.

December 2006

As I begin to conclude this journey in 2006, on December 13, I played tennis with a Cornel, a neighborhood friend. I spotted him four games to make it fun and won seven straight games to win the match. While playing, Cornel told me he was the seventh son, born on July 7.

As I conclude my clue seeking for 2006 and end this chapter, I still ask myself, "What is the significance of significance, and does it ever end?" The number thirteen still resonates in my life but I have observed many occurrences of the number seven. In fact, seven will be the revelation for 2007 and I will again record the fascination with the clues I have been given. For example, I entered the Atlanta 2007 Summer Men's 4.5 Singles Tournament, and I won the championship. The journey will continue in part two of *Clue Seekers*. Chapter 13 will summarize the meaning of the events in my personal life and shed light on the importance of creating your own oasis.

Chapter 13

The New Beginning: Create Your Oasis

You have read a fascinating journey of excitement, mystery, and intrigue. I hope you find the meaning in your life from the signs and symbols all around you. I tried to be a catalyst for your awareness. As I was going through these experiences, two movies were circulating that summed up the mysterious force into which I suggest you tap. One is called *What the Bleep Do We Know?* The other movie is *The Secret*. There is a follow up to the first movie called *Down the Rabbit Hole*, and each is recommended for you to fully understand this journey called life. These contemporary films will help familiarize you with how we view ourselves.

I was in search of an identity, already aware that identity was at the root of many of the problems that exist. As I transformed my consciousness, I no longer viewed myself as just an African because I no longer could accurately define what it meant to be African. I tried to understand what makes an African, European, Asian, Indian . . . Were these distinctions why there is so much disconnect? Identity helps provide clarity for those who cannot identify with the spiritual component.

Most people are selfish by nature, and that could be why identity is critical for a positive outlook. There is strife because many people are xenophobic and unable to appreciate differences. I love, appreciate, honor, and respect people of color, but that does not mean that I disrespect people who lack color. Culture and/or ethnicity complicate the commonalities between people. After four decades of life, I feel more accommodating of others who do not look like me. I see a greater development for positive human relations when we focus on the mind as the part of the commonality.

I believe the mind is the final frontier, and we must gain control of our thoughts and merge as one collective consciousness to seek true peace and happiness. In order for the world to change, a new thought must be ushered in, grasped, and utilized by the human mind. Most people do not want to change and that is perhaps why I refused to see the problems in my marriage.

What the Bleep Do We Know? brought attention to one factor affecting the mental problems my ex-spouse was having. I had an attraction for a woman in 1999; my mate found out. I acknowledged the attraction and reiterated that no sexual intercourse had occurred. To me, it was over, done, and time to move away from the drama, but she was stuck in the past.

For years, I had no idea what was wrong with my mate. Misery loves company, and maybe she expected me to live in her hell. She had no lock and chain on her. If she desired to look for another man/woman to be in her life, she was never held back. Instead of love and forgiveness, she generated hate and revenge. I maintained the premise that I was not going to live in uncertainty. Her broken mind was not going to deter me. Allow unhappy people to live in their own hell; do not make their reality your own.

Love triangles are dangerous. I chose to walk away. Read the news; how many individuals can humbly walk away from drama? Domestic violence, cheating, divorce, and death are the result of love triangles. People make wrong decisions when their emotions are unbalanced. I focused on my children and being a responsible husband and father.

For my children to have no father because he killed a man or to have no mother was not imaginable. I chose not to take her to court and mention her affair because she could have lost her job. I tried to move beyond emotional pettiness and not expose her activities. I walked out of divorce court with my dignity and character intact, and my children will have as supportive a life from me as I can provide under the circumstances. The judge ordered me to pay child support; it is as if their mother was rewarded for having an extramarital affair. This sort of outcome can cause a man to hate his ex-wife. I say only that if you know what happiness is, do the best you can to remain in it. People searching for happiness will never find it. You must be happy with yourself then your life can become synchronistic.

After my revelations, I became more aware of the forces guiding me. Amanda, the main character in *What the Bleep Do We Know*, was on medication, confused, and stuck in the past. When you cannot change, you die. You should always search for growth and development. When you seek revenge and retribution, your life is headed for hell. Hell is your life gone wrong. When you feel as though your life is going wrong—change directions. I believe the symbols were and have been shown to me via ancestors, the cosmic force, and/or the creator. Whatever you call it, do not resist trying to understand the signs.

As I was bombarded with clue after clue, I transformed my consciousness and changed my outlook on life. I feel I have become more compassionate of other people's feelings. Respect others and never assume that you would respond as another would until you are in their shoes.

I remember a colleague whose two-year-old daughter was raped at day care. He was accused by Social Services of raping his own daughter. He sat in jail and went to trial to prove that he did not. It was a terrible injustice. I recall a similar scenario from *A Time to Kill,* and I believe I would have physically harmed the perpetrator if it were my daughter.

My colleague had the moral restraint not to carry out an act of violence. I did not walk in his path, but I emotionally felt that I would have harmed the perpetrator. Perhaps his stance gave me strength and restraint in my circumstance. I know some people would have responded with an act of violence toward their spouse if he or she cheated on them. Always think about the consequences of your actions before you make an emotional response.

This book is not written to repair broken minds. This book is written to celebrate life and to encourage a new way of thinking. Get out of the box and see what the world has to offer. If you are stuck, wake up; the world is changing. It may be good or it may be bad, but change is coming. You have a precious role to play in life. No person is too small to affect a change. Your view is not the only one. See what life has to offer. Read literature that uplifts your spirit. Throw away media that sends your emotions out of control. Be in control of your life.

I do not claim to have all of the answers, but I do know that the solution is in the mind. When you do not control your own thinking, you are bound to be led to a place you should not be. Search for clues that will set you on the correct path. The answers are there. Some are hidden, some are right in front of you, and either way, there is a message that moves you forward. Life is all about growth and development.

No matter what culture, language, ethnicity, or gender you may be, the commonality of the universe we live in makes our experiences similar. I hope my life experience will help you to pay attention to the clues that show direction in your life. You have to want life to live, and many people are scared to live. Seek the answers; we will all be waiting for your contribution.

It sounds easy, but it is not. Creating your own oasis may be the most challenging aspect of life because many times, the first thought is, "I can't." *Clue Seeker* reminds you to think forward forever and backward never.

Epilogue

Traveling overseas can present circumstances not under your control. Although my excursion to Africa and Portugal ended with a safe journey home, I missed a connecting flight in London on my return to Atlanta. The mistake was due to miscommunication with the airline representative in London. When I finally arrived in the U.S., I was held over at customs. If my connecting flight in the U.S. had not been delayed due to bad weather, I would have missed my flight from New Jersey to Georgia. I would have been stranded in Newark, NJ.

I felt fortunate that I landed safely in America when I was scheduled to arrive. I was safe and secure, and I had choices. Even if I had missed my connecting flight in Newark, NJ, I was prepared to rent a car and drive home. In London, I missed both my connecting flights, and it was frustrating because I had no choices. If the airline had said there were no available flights until two or three days later, I would have been stranded. I had no direct flights to any destinations, so I was asking for hassles.

I emphasize my circuitous but fortunate return because of the information shared with me about my E-Project team and their scheduled return. I called my roommate T. Scott in California to find out how the E-Project turned out for my colleagues. We were all scheduled to arrive home on a Friday. I was coming from Portugal, and they were returning from Ghana. I called his home two days after my return to give him time to get settled. I spoke to his friend Stacy, and we had a lengthy conversation, as if we both had known one another for years. Since T. Scott and I spent ten days as roommates, we got to know plenty about one another. I was shocked to hear that he had not yet returned home. Stacy told me that Ghana Airways had been shut down. She said that the U.S. government officially grounded all Ghana Airway flights. I was shocked. How could this be? How could the entire contingent of E-Project ambassadors be stuck on the continent against their will? There was no certainty of when they would return.

I prayed for their safety and waited for information on how everyone was managing. Whatever I had experienced suddenly became trivial. My comrades could not rent a car or boat to return to their families. I thought about their families and the worry that must have been on everyone's mind. You can become extremely depressed having no control over your destiny. I thought about how our ancestors were forcibly taken and removed from Africa centuries ago; these modern day Africans were forced to remain in Africa.

Fortunately, the E-Project crew arrived one week later with relatively peaceful spirits. I finally spoke to T. Scott and he told me that everyone on the trip just dealt with the disappointment. Everyone was a trooper and supported one another.

I have shared the E-Project experience with friends, family, and students, and they were astonished by Africa. I have done my part to pass on my experience, and each of us has gone back to our communities to spread the word about reconnecting with Africa. Two years after my trip to Ghana and Portugal, I traveled to Salvador, Brazil to serve as an E-Project ambassador. T. Scott and I landed below the equator in February 2006, and I returned for a solo mission in July. We established lasting relationships with the students and personnel at the Steve Biko Institute. It was great to provide education for those with a thirst for knowledge.

The Brazilian airlines on which I flew, Varig, went bankrupt while I was visiting. Varig offered no recourse, and no representative could tell me when there would be flights to my destination. I could have been stuck for days. The experience of my E-Project colleagues two years prior had prepared me for the ordeal. My colleagues were stuck in Africa for a week. I was stuck in a foreign land with no support from the administration. I was stranded and in search of a clue. Although I had to pay extra, I made it home on the thirteenth day of my excursion. I had a wonderful time for thirteen days, and I began to ask myself where home is. I had been in clue seeker mode for some time, and I reflected on the message I was to learn. How could an entire airline just shut down and leave hundreds of travelers stranded? Perhaps my happiness and joy is below the equator; perhaps that is where my future lies. Life is a journey; follow the clues, and never give up.

CPSIA information can be obtained
at www.ICGtesting.com
Printed in the USA
FFHW021931210819
54453120-60139FF